Meet Simone Biles

INSPIRATIONAL BIOGRAPHIES FOR KIDS WITH BIG DREAMS

by Poppy Wilder

Janey
Merry Christmas!
2024
From,
Jenny

© Copyright 2024 Blisshouse Publishing - All rights reserved.

The content contained within this book may not be reproduced, duplicated or transmitted without direct written permission from the author or the publisher.

Under no circumstances will any blame or legal responsibility be held against the publisher, or author, for any damages, reparation, or monetary loss due to the information contained within this book, either directly or indirectly.

Legal Notice:

This book is copyright protected. It is only for personal use. You cannot amend, distribute, sell, use, quote or paraphrase any part, or the content within this book, without the consent of the author or publisher.

Disclaimer Notice:

Please note the information contained within this document is for educational and entertainment purposes only. All effort has been executed to present accurate, up to date, reliable, complete information. No warranties of any kind are declared or implied. Readers acknowledge that the author is not engaged in the rendering of legal, financial, medical or professional advice. The content within this book has been derived from various sources. Please consult a licensed professional before attempting any techniques outlined in this book.

By reading this document, the reader agrees that under no circumstances is the author responsible for any losses, direct or indirect, that are incurred as a result of the use of the information contained within this document, including, but not limited to, errors, omissions, or inaccuracies.

ISBN paperback: 978-1-963131-05-5
ISBN eBook: 978-1-963131-06-2

To Nova,

May every twist, turn, and tumble become a new chapter in your journey towards greatness.

Love,
Mom

CONTENTS	PAGES
Introduction: Meet Simone Biles!	7-10
Chapter 1: Tiny Tumbler's Beginnings	11-18
Chapter 2: Flips and Frustrations	19-25
Chapter 3: From Challenges to Championships	26-34
Chapter 4: Unleashing the Superstar	25-40
Chapter 5: Conquering the Inner Balance Beam	41-48
Chapter 6: Gold-medal Glory	49-54
Chapter 7: Giving Back and Inspiring Others	55-62
Chapter 8: The Sky's the Limit	63-70
Chapter 9: Believe in Your Personal Power!	71-73
Chapter 10: Timeline of Simone's Successes	74-76
Conclusion: Your Journey Starts Here	77-78
Glossary	79-80
References	81-82

INTRODUCTION

Simone Biles shines brightly in the world of gymnastics. She's not just a champion; she's a role model who inspires people all around the globe. From a young girl with big dreams to a record-breaking gymnast, Simone's journey is filled with determination, hard work, and the belief that anything is possible.

MEET SIMONE BILES!

Before she became a four-time **Olympic** gold medalist, Simone was a 6-year-old child with dreams bigger than any balance beam could support. She was the unstoppable athletic force who dominated her first Olympic division of artistic gymnastics in the 2013 Olympic Games at Rio de Janeiro, Brazil, and was still winning competitions 10 years later. Beyond her balance-beam dreams, Simone continued to inspire others to reach their own personal greatness by being **empathetic**, **resilient**, and willing to stand up for themselves the way she stood up for herself. She wouldn't be kept down or held back!

THE ART OF GYMNASTICS

Gymnastics is the umbrella term used for the division of athletics where a person strengthens their body so they can perform rhythmic and graceful exercises. Balance beams, uneven bars, gym mats, rings, a vaulting horse, or pommel might be used for different gymnastics **routines**. The sport requires a great deal of coordination, **agility**, focus, and daily practice to make sure the gymnast doesn't get hurt while performing.

The average gymnast spends about 20 hours each week training to perform at the highest levels. In the beginning, new participants should spend under five hours in the gym each week to strengthen their muscles and learn the more challenging routines.

TRAIN HARD, WORK HARD

Becoming an Olympian takes oodles of dedication. These top-tier athletes usually start training when they are under age 5 so that their bodies develop the muscle tone, strength, and support required to compete. Anyone who dreams of being a champion will need to put their training and education first. Downtime, friends, and fun usually fill in the few hours that remain after a long day of training and schoolwork.

Rest is also an important part of the training process. Did you know that when you sleep your body repairs itself? When your body and mind are at rest, the sore muscles you use all day become stronger again.

FUN FACT

Taking care of an athletic body can be tough work! Eating a healthy diet of vegetables, fruit, lean protein, and whole grains helps athletes maintain enough energy to fuel their performances. Athletes avoid injury by using massage, hydrotherapy, and stretching before and after their routines to ease the transition from performance to rest.

DID YOU KNOW?

There are different levels of gymnastic ability. Pre-team gymnasts are beginners and toddlers. Levels two through five are not as skilled as levels six through 10. Elite gymnasts are the highest level of competitors and spend the most time training, up to 70 hours each and every week!

INSPIRATIONAL QUOTE:

"We also have to focus on ourselves, because at the end of the day, we're human, too. We have to protect our mind and our body, rather than just go out there and do what the world wants us to do," Simone told reporters at US Weekly (Nardino, 2023).

Hello Inspiration

In these sections throughout the book, you are invited to dream big and journal answers to questions that get your mind moving. You'll find a variety of topics to explore as inspired by Simone, herself. Remember to have fun!

CHAPTER 1: A TINY TUMBLER'S BEGINNINGS

LEAPING INTO LIFE

On the way to becoming a successful gymnast, Simone stumbled over many circumstances in her early life. Her mother was unable to care for Simone or her siblings so Simone's grandparents stepped in to help. Simone went to live with them permanently when she was only 6.

A CHAMPION IS BORN

On March 14, 1997, Simone Arianne Biles was born in Columbus, Ohio. She was the third of four children, but her biological mother and father could not overcome their addictions. Simone and her sister, Adria, were adopted and raised

by her mom's parents, Nellie and Ronald Biles, in Texas. Her two older brothers, Adam and Ronald, went to live with their great-aunt.

EARLY SPARKLES

Shortly after being taken in by her grandparents at the age of 6, Simone went with her daycare on a field trip to a gymnastics center. She immediately fell in love with the artistry of gymnastics that she saw performed at Bannon's Gymnastix in Houston, Texas.

Simone began to believe that with her new start she also would be capable of performing the aerial feats she saw being performed at the gym. It was a topic of in-depth discussion at dinner that night because the coach who saw her trying out her own gymnastics moves on the mats had sent a letter home recommending she try gymnastics for real. She asked if she could start lessons, and her grandparents agreed!

DREAMING BIG

Simone took gymnastics seriously and trained as often as she could. Her high energy, fearless nature, and strength at such a young age helped her stand out from others in her class. She excelled at every event she tried.

However, having all that energy came with a struggle to sit still and focus on her schoolwork. Simone was diagnosed with attention deficit hyperactivity disorder (ADHD) around this same time (Simone Biles: Gymnast and Olympic gold medalist, 2023). This diagnosis did not slow Simone down. In fact, it encouraged her to work harder to concentrate whenever she needed to be still. She trained her mind in this way while she was also training her body for Olympic greatness.

FUN FACT

Simone likes dogs and prefers German shepherds. She has had as many as four, including her childhood pup named Maggie. Others she's had have included Lilly, Atlas, and Bella.

DID YOU KNOW?

Nellie and Ron are Simone's parents. She has no problem correcting anyone who suggests that these two life-changing individuals are just her grandparents.

INSPIRATIONAL QUOTE:

"My parents are my parents and that's it," Simone told a reporter who'd accidentally called her parents "grandparents" during an interview at her first Olympic competition (Escobar, 2021). It is okay to correct someone politely when they make a mistake.

Hello Inpiration 1

Imagine meeting Simone Biles. What questions would you ask her?

Hello Inspiration 2

Have you watched or practiced gymnastics? What are some of your favorite things about gymnastics?

Hello Inspiration 3

Draw a picture of yourself meeting Simone Biles for the first time.

CHAPTER 2: FLIPS AND FRUSTRATIONS

UPS AND DOWNS

Simone's first coach, Aimee Boorman, had never trained an elite athlete before, so she and Simone learned together exactly what makes a champion. Training was intense, but getting an education always came first. When Simone's ADHD made focusing on schoolwork difficult, Simone's parents asked doctors what else could be done to help Simone.

They prescribed medication for Simone that would help her settle down enough to get her work done.

By training her mind to slow down, focus, and concentrate on the task at hand, and now with the help of a doctor-approved medication, Simone was able to complete her studies for the day and spend time training her body. She worked hard after school for five years, and in 2011, at the age of 14, she earned third place in her first national competition, the American Classic in Houston (Simone Biles: Gymnast and Olympic gold medalist, 2023).

After this victory, Simone decided to trade her usual school routine for working hard full-time in the gym. Her parents started homeschooling Simone when she was 14 years old. Gymnastics training became her full-time job, and she worked hard for up to eight hours each day.

Even though the decision meant Simone would never go to prom or spend time doing other social activities that teens often experience, she hasn't regretted her decision. She made several friends on her gymnastics teams and she traveled the world more than most people her age.

After all that intensive training, the 2012 American Classic was more successful for Simone and her team. She placed:

- 1st in the all-around competition
- 1st on the vault
- 2nd in floor exercise
- 3rd on the balance beam

These accomplishments proved her strength and her determination to be a fierce competitor. The USA Gymnastics National Championships were also that year. Simone's first place in the vault competition secured her a spot on the United States

Junior National Team which would go on to compete in the Olympics. However, at 15 she was still too young to compete on an Olympic team. The youngest a person can be is 16.

Simone kept practicing and continued to enter other competitions to prepare for the next Olympic Games in 2016. In the meantime, Simone took on the 2013 American Cup in Texas and then competed with her team for the City of Jesolo Trophy in Italy, where she secured four gold medal wins!

THE COURAGE TO CONTINUE

However, in 2013 Simone also experienced a crushing defeat as she fell from the balance beam at the American Classic competition. The pain of such a public disappointment seemed to take its toll on her mental health. She felt like a failure.

Her coach set up some meetings with one of the world's premier gymnastics coaches, Márta Károlyi, which seemed to get Simone back on track. She was able to block out the expectations of others and focus on the joy of gymnastics once again.

In her first competition three weeks after her fall, Simone came back stronger and more sure than ever. She was back, this time appointed to the Senior National Team. Her next wins came in Belgium at the World Gymnastics Championships. These merits included:
- 1st in all-around competition
- 1st in floor exercise
- 2nd on the vault
- and the first international title of her career!

DID YOU KNOW?

She has five gymnastics moves, known as elements, named after her! Her first one came after her floor exercise routine for the 2013 World Championships. "The Biles" was performed with a small change to the landing position of the double layout by "executing a half-twist and landing on one foot" (Simone Biles: Gymnast and Olympic gold medalist, 2023). Her coach suggested this alteration to prevent further injury to her already sore knee from her performances on the vault and balance beam earlier in the same competition.

INSPIRATIONAL QUOTE:

"I am not the next Usain Bolt or Michael Phelps. I am the first Simone Biles," Simone said during an interview directly after her first gold-medal Olympic win in Rio de Janeiro, Brazil. She wanted to set the record straight that she is blazing a path for girls and women everywhere (Reynolds, 2016).

Hello Inspiration 4

Think of a time when you faced a challenge or obstacle in your life.
How did it make you feel, and what did you do to overcome it?

Hello Inspiration 5

Imagine you're an athlete like Simone Biles. What would your daily routine look like?

Hello Inspiration 6

Imagine you have a magic wand that can help you overcome any challenge.
Draw a picture of this wand and on the handle, write words that encourage you and build your confidence.

CHAPTER 3: FROM CHALLENGES TO CHAMPIONSHIPS

PUSHING BOUNDARIES

Simone never shied away from a challenge. When she let the crowd and everyone else's expectations get to her, she fell off the balance beam. When she missed the birthdate cutoff for the 2012 Olympics only by a few months, she was disappointed but she kept training. She entered many other competitions until the Olympics came around again.

And in 2016, when she was finally old enough to compete in her first Olympics, she dominated in every competition she entered. Since the rating system changed from being on a 10-point scale to including merit for difficulty, Simone stepped outside her comfort zone and pushed her gymnastics limits.

This choice paid off for her because she won four gold medals. She won golds on the vault, in the all-around, for the team, and on the floor event. It was the bronze medal she earned on the balance beam, however, that made her want to work harder to win all gold medals at the next Olympic Games.

OVERCOMING FEAR

The fear of failure can stop anyone from chasing their dreams. You might feel like your dreams are silly or not realistic. But, like Simone, don't ever let that stop you from trying. Fall off the balance beam six times, but get back up seven times!

Train, practice, and focus on your dreams. Each tiny step will bring you that much closer than standing still will. You'll come back from any challenge stronger and more determined than ever.

The next time Simone entered a competition, her performance defied the laws of gravity—and it was flawless. But others tried to take her hard-earned medals away from her.

Shortly after the 2016 Olympic Games ended, computer hackers accessed and released personal information about Simone. They hoped that the medication she took for ADHD would **disqualify** her and strip her of her medals. Some medicines, when found in an athlete's bloodstream, go against the rules for athletic performance in competitions. This can ruin a person's career and reputation.

Simone faced the criticism head-on. She was honest about her **diagnosis**. Even though her personal information was out there for everyone to know, the effect was the opposite of what the hackers wished. The medication was within the rules. She kept her medals, and she inspired others to open up about their own medical issues, to not feel like they have to hide their challenges in similar situations.

FUN FACT

During the iconic closing ceremony for the 2016 Rio de Janeiro Olympic Games, Simone was chosen to hold the flag for her country and her team. This is an honor that recognizes her contribution to USA's epic win that year.

DID YOU KNOW?

There are two traditional versions of the Olympics—one that takes place in the winter and one that happens in the summer. Each highlights the athletic talents of competitors from around the world for sports that are played either during warmer months or colder ones. Both occur once every four years, so some type of Olympics happens every two years. Other athletes participate in the Paralympic Games, which feature athletes who are differently-abled— such as using a wheelchair or having a prosthetic limb—competing in adapted versions of various events.

INSPIRATIONAL QUOTE:

"I just hope that kids growing up watching this don't or aren't ashamed of being good at whatever they do. And that's my problem: when people kind of harp on other people that are good at something. And it's like, everybody can say you're good, but once you acknowledge it, it's not cool anymore. And I want kids to learn that, yes, it's okay to acknowledge that you're good or even great at something," Simone told Marie Claire magazine (Igoe, 2021).

Hello Inspiration 7

Imagine you're a gymnast like Simone Biles competing at the highest level.
What would be your favorite part of performing on national and international stages?

Hello Inspiration 8

What would you do to get ready for a gymnastics performance?
What would you eat, how often would you practice, and what positive things would you tell yourself?

Hello Inspiration 9

Draw a picture of yourself performing a gymnastics routine at a national championship.

CHAPTER 4: UNLEASHING THE SUPERSTAR

MASTERING THE SKILLS

Now that Simone had made a name for herself on a worldwide scale, she was ready to put her stardom to good use. She chose to take 711 days off (almost two full years!) between her win in 2016 and her return to the gym mats in July 2018. She took the time to rest her mind and her body. She'd been pushing limits for 13 years! To avoid burnout and fatigue, Simone needed to find balance. She also used this time to help others. When Simone came back into the public eye, she soared above the competition.

Public speaking hadn't been much of a challenge for Simone. She'd been honest about her struggles with ADHD and focusing on one task at a time. She also opened up about her experience being abused by the former doctor for the US Olympics gymnastics team. He hurt at least 150 athletes in his time as a doctor there and Simone was among the first to call on the Olympics committee to do something about it.

When you know something is wrong, speaking up is important. Talk to someone you trust, such as a parent, teacher, or adult friend who can help.

PRACTICE MAKES PERFECT

The more you practice speaking up for yourself, the easier it will be to speak your truth. You might feel like butterflies are fluttering in your tummy or your heart is beating fast, but speak up anyway.

Afterward, you will feel a sense of relief that you did the right thing even when it wasn't easy. In everything you do, step out of your comfort zone and face your fears to achieve your goals even when you're afraid.

FUN FACT

In July, August, and November of 2018, Simone competed at the US Classic, the USA Gymnastics National Championships, and the World Gymnastics Championships. She won gold medals in each event she entered! These included her first gold medal in the uneven bars, and golds in balance beam, floor, all-around, vault, and in her team final for a total of 13 medals in under four months!

DID YOU KNOW?

During her participation in the 2018 World Gymnastics Championships, Simone was battling the excruciating pain of having a kidney stone. Kidney stones are small particles inside the body that can accumulate in the urinary tract where urine, or pee, is passed. They can be as small as a grain of sand, but they cause intense pain as they pass through the body. Simone refused to take any pain medicine while performing because they would have gone against the rules of the competition. She would have been disqualified, so she pushed through—and won anyway.

INSPIRATIONAL QUOTE:

"I was like, 'Sorry, I have to compete so I'm leaving, but thanks for letting me know I have a kidney stone and I'll deal with the pain later!'" Simone gleefully told the nursing staff at the hospital when she was told she might have to stay for observation instead of continuing to compete (Praderio, 2018).

Hello Inspiration 10

Imagine you're a gymnast.
What skill would you be most excited to master, and why?

Hello Inspiration 11

Write about a time when you dedicated yourself to learning a new skill or subject.
How did your determination help you succeed?

Hello Inspiration 12

Draw a picture of a star. Inside the star, list your natural talents and things you are good at doing. If they don't all fit in one star, add some more!

CHAPTER 5: CONQUERING THE INNER BALANCE BEAM

FACING FEARS

A healthy body starts with a healthy mind. Simone Biles was never one to shy away from talking about the importance of facing mental health issues, even in the face of criticism and stigmas surrounding this topic. When the 2020 Olympics in Tokyo, Japan, came around, Simone was unsure of herself.

STRENGTH FROM WITHIN

Sometimes, even the greatest athletes of all time need to take a break to refocus. Simone had pushed through pain for most of her career, and that courage earned her great applause and awards. But then she nearly fell during her vault set in Tokyo. She wasn't injured, but she took the near miss as a warning that she needed to slow down, breathe, and gather herself or risk losing control. As the world watched, Simone decided to sit out of all other events she had signed up to take on, and cheered on her teammates instead. During the final day of competition, she made a triumphant return in the final event—the balance beam—and won bronze.

Simone's withdrawal reminded us that she's just human, and that even when you want something so badly that it's all you can see, you have to remind yourself from time to time to slow your movements and focus on the moment. This will help you reach your ultimate goal in a much healthier way than blazing through every time. Putting your own well-being first will help you go farther than if you just push through. Life isn't always about winning.

FUN FACT

Sometimes gymnasts get what they call the "twisties," where their mental and physical health are imbalanced. They lose their sense of where they are in the air and this could lead to a dangerous inability to land correctly. To fix twisties, extensive training for the mind and the body needs to happen at the same time so that the gymnast can untangle their feelings to get back on track. Simone went through this during her first event at the Tokyo Olympics even as an elite gymnast. No one is immune to the pressures of performing.

DID YOU KNOW?

Simone talked about how the connection between her body and mind is affected by different kinds of pain. Physical pain for athletes can take four to six weeks to heal. This kind of injury is often visible. However, emotional pain is not something everyone can see easily. This kind of pain takes longer to process or think through. She said, "There's, like, no time limit or healing time for it, so you just take it day by day" (Nardino, 2023). Not all pain is apparent, so it's important to be kind to everyone you meet because you never know what they're going through.

INSPIRATIONAL QUOTE:

"I definitely feel like it's been a relief [to speak openly about my emotions], but it's not easy to go through it because I try to be strong not only for other people but also myself. But sometimes there are weaknesses in strength and that's okay. And it's okay not to be okay, and I've taught myself that," Simone said, explaining her realization in a 2021 interview (Nardino, 2023). She keeps her mind and body healthy by recognizing when she needs a break and when she's okay to push through.

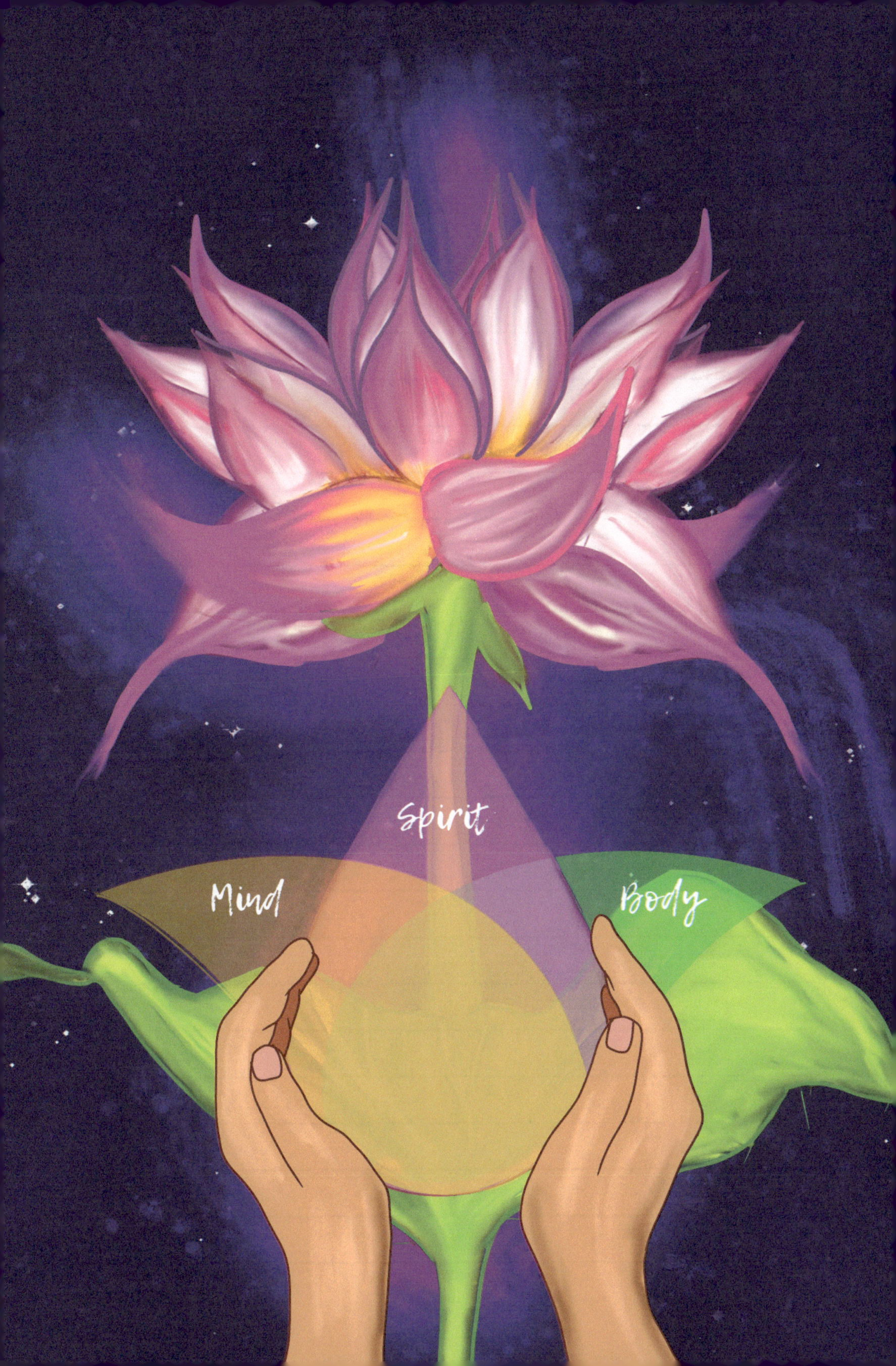
Spirit
Mind
Body

Hello Inspiration 13

What are three things you love about yourself? How can these qualities help you stay confident?

Hello Inspiration 14

When you are sad or frustrated, what are three things or activities that help you feel calm and relaxed?

Hello Inspiration 15

Draw a picture of yourself doing one of the activities that helps you feel the most calm and relaxed.

CHAPTER 6: GOLD-MEDAL GLORY

OLYMPIC TRIUMPH

Simone is the most decorated gymnast in the history of the sport. The long road to success began when she was only 6 years old, but she kept that momentum going for more than 20 years. She competed in two Olympic games and earned four gold, one silver, and two bronze medals by the time she was 26.

The gymnastics skills that have been named after her include five different moves: The Biles on the balance beam; the Biles and Biles II on the vault; and the Biles and Biles II on the floor. Simone continues to impress the judges at every competition she enters as a senior international elite artistic gymnast.

ACHIEVING DREAMS

After 20 years of training, competing, and taking on the gymnastics world, Simone didn't show any signs of slowing down. As of October 2023, she had won 34 medals from her efforts at the World Gymnastics Championships. She also secured a fifth gymnastics move named after her on October 14, 2023, when she performed the Biles II on the vault. Ten years prior to this amazing honor, she had had her first gymnastics feat named after her in the same arena. Her career had come full circle and Simone was extremely proud of all she'd accomplished.

FUN FACT

The National Governing Board of Gymnastics is the group responsible for naming gymnastic skills after the athlete who performs them.

Did You Know?

In the 2016 Olympic Games in Rio, Simone was the shortest of all the 555 competitors from all over the world. At 4 feet 8 inches tall, she does not tower over the competition, but she still commands respect in each of her events. She doesn't let her height stop her. She uses her physical characteristics, like being short and muscular, to win!

INSPIRATIONAL QUOTE:

"Growing up, I didn't see very many Black gymnasts ... So whenever I did, I felt really inspired to go out there and want to be as good as them. I remember watching Gabby Douglas win the 2012 Olympics, and I was like, If she can do it, I can do it," Simone told reporters, explaining what inspired her to follow her passion (Igoe, 2021).

Hello Inspiration 16

What is a dream you would like to achieve?

Hello Inspiration 17

What is something you can do to move yourself closer to achieving your dream?

Hello Inspiration 18

Draw a picture of a gold medal with your name on it.
What achievement does it represent, and how does it make you feel?

CHAPTER 7: GIVING BACK AND INSPIRING OTHERS

MAKING A DIFFERENCE

In 2018, Simone was dealing with a heavy sadness. While she'd always been open about how pushing herself to the limits had affected her mental health, she didn't want to talk publicly about something she experienced behind closed doors. She thought about other gymnasts who were coming forward about a doctor for the USA team who was harming the girls. She eventually came to terms with understanding that what had happened wasn't right.

Simone used her status as an Olympic powerhouse to bring awareness to abuse. Her voice gave other survivors the courage to speak out about what happened to them.

THE JOY OF GIVING

In addition to speaking out about wrongs, this Olympic champion regularly gave back to her community by donating money and time to help children in the foster care system. Not many resources are available to the estimated 391,000 children under age 18 who are without parents or guardians to care for them (How many kids are in foster care in the US?, 2023). Simone's work with the Friends of the Children organization helps children gain the mental, emotional, and personal strength to overcome what happened in their past so that they can create dreams and chase a brighter future.

Simone thrived in life because she had someone who believed in her. This gave her the courage to believe in herself. She made it all the way to Olympic greatness. Simone believed that everyone deserves a chance at a great life. So she gave as much of her time, energy, and effort as she possibly could to be that inspirational driving force for others

For as much time as Simone spent training in the gym, she also tried to make a difference in other children's lives. One example of this important principle to Simone was when she helped Mattress Firm gift new beds with fresh sheets to children who had been in a homeless shelter in Garland, Texas. This shelter, Jonathan's Place, housed foster children who had been hurt and abandoned. Simone's hope was that the new beds would help

these children dream up new beginnings and "dream big" (Walker, 2018). Each time she reached out to children, Simone hoped they would see how she was once in foster care, and she still became a gold medalist. Maybe her story will help inspire you, too!

FUN FACT

As the youngest person to ever receive the Presidential Medal of Freedom, Simone was only 25 years old when President Joe Biden presented her with this honor for her work with children in the foster care system. The award also recognized her outstanding athletic abilities and her mental health **advocacy**.

DID YOU KNOW?

As of October 2023, Simone had won the most world championship gold medals (an astounding 21!) of any gymnast in the history of the sport. Her wins in 2023 put her in the spotlight once again. She became the oldest gymnast to earn eight US all-around titles and she won her sixth international all-around title, as well (Simone Biles: Gymnast and Olympic gold medalist, 2023).

INSPIRATIONAL QUOTE:

"After hearing the brave stories of my friends and other survivors, I know that this horrific experience does not define me. I am much more than this. I am unique, smart, talented, motivated, and passionate. I have promised myself that my story will be much greater than this and I promise all of you that I will never give up … I won't let one man, and the others that enabled him, to steal my love and joy," Simone tweeted to show anyone going through trauma that life will get better (Igoe, 2021).

Hello Inspiration 19

Imagine you have a magic wand that can grant one wish to make the world a better place. What would your wish be and why?

Hello Inspiration 20

Create a list of three small acts of kindness you can perform this week to brighten someone's day.

1.

2.

3.

Hello Inspiration 21

Draw a picture of yourself helping others and being an inspiration in your community. What does helping look like and how does it make you feel?

CHAPTER 8:
THE SKY'S THE LIMIT

LOOKING AHEAD TO WHAT THE FUTURE HOLDS

Even with all her medals and awards, Simone continued to build her legacy of perseverance. At 26 years old, she made history by being the first woman to perform a Yurchenko double pike on the vault. She knew she would lose a half-point if she had her coach spot her as she performed the death-defying maneuver. However, Simone's performance was still enough to beat the competition and she proved to

herself that she could make her dreams come true. The complicated move was renamed the Biles II, and it became the fifth skill with Simone's name on it. Simone was more determined than ever to keep her winning streak going.

    Simone's fiercest competition had always been herself. Although she won silver for the difficult stunt in this event, Simone was proud of her efforts. The half-point deduction was enough to make the gold medal barely out of reach. "All in all, I don't think it will hit me until maybe I retire and then look back and see everything that I've done. Tonight, I think it was a good start," Simone said about everything she accomplished throughout her time as a gymnast (Armour, 2023).

DREAMING BIG LIKE SIMONE

Simone didn't let anything stand in her way. Injuries, getting married, and overcoming stress were no match for Simone. After competing in the Tokyo Olympics, she took time off and she returned to compete in the August 2023 Core Hydration Classic. She blew the other competitors out of the water by scoring five points higher than the second- and third-best gymnasts.

    In October 2023, Simone followed up her previous big win with her work on the balance beam. This had been her weakest event, but she won the gold medal in this and the floor exercise events at the FIG Artistic World Championships. Each time she takes a break from competition, she comes back stronger and more determined to win.

FUN FACT

Many people refer to Simone as the GOAT, which stands for the Greatest of All Time. That means her determination and unmatched athletic abilities are recognized as being at the highest level. Balancing her health and her dreams of winning put her above every other gymnast.

DID YOU KNOW?

Simone married an NFL football player named Jonathan Owens in April 2023. They met online during her second break from sports in 2020.

INSPIRATIONAL QUOTE:

"Personally, for me, I don't think of it as an obligation ... I think of it as an honor to speak for the less fortunate and for the voiceless. I also feel like it gives them power," Simone said as a way to bring awareness to issues that affect everyone, including Olympic gold medal winners (Igoe, 2021).

Hello Inspiration 22

What inspired you most about Simone Biles's story?

Hello Inpiration 23

Who are some other people who inspire you? How do they inspire you?

Hello Inspiration 24

Draw a picture of you and Simone Biles doing one of your favorite activities together.

YOU CAN DO IT, TOO

In a short amount of time, Simone overcame adversity, earned several Olympic gold medals and other gold, silver, and bronze medals, and inspired generations to chase their dreams. After her two-year hiatus, she returned to competition stronger and more determined than ever!

Always chase your dreams, even if they seem to be taking a long time to reach.

MAKE A COLLAGE OF MAGAZINE CUTOUTS TO CREATE A VISION BOARD OF YOUR GOALS AS YOU ASPIRE TO INSPIRE LIKE

Simone.

CHAPTER 10:

March 1997: Simone Biles is born in Columbus, Ohio.

Early 2003: Simone and her sister, Adria, are adopted by their maternal grandparents, who live in Spring, Texas, a suburb of Houston.

2013: At the World Championships, Simone takes home two gold medals and an all-around title. This ensures that everyone knows her name; she's an unstoppable force.

Sometime around 2000: Simone and her siblings are placed in foster care in the state of Ohio because their parents cannot care for them.

Late 2003: On her first trip to a gymnastics center with her daycare in Texas, Simone falls in love with the artistry of gymnastics.

2014: This time, she won four gold medals at the World Championships.

TIMELINE OF SIMONE'S SUCCESSES

2015: Simone wins another four gold medals at the World Championships.

2017: She wins the ESPY Award for Best Female Athlete of the Year.

2016: Simone wins big at the Olympics in Rio de Janeiro with four gold medals (one with her team and individual medals on the vault, all-around, and on the floor exercise). She also won one bronze medal for her balance beam work.

2018: Simone takes home four gold medals at the USA Gymnastics National Championships. This is also the year that Simone and other gymnasts face their fears to testify in court about their abuser, Larry Nassar, who used to be a doctor for Team USA. She went on to win in each event in the U.S. Classic and the World Gymnastics Championships that same year.

July-August 2021:
The 2020 Tokyo Olympics were a challenge for Simone, but she still won silver with her team and bronze for her balance beam event. These were her sixth and seventh Olympic medals. The international competition was held a year after it was scheduled due to safety concerns during the global COVID-19 pandemic.

April 2023:
Simone Biles and Jonathan Owens are married. Simone's last name is now Biles Owens.

July 18, 2022:
President Joe Biden awards Simone the Presidential Medal of Freedom.

October 2023:
At the US Classic, Simone shows no signs of stopping as she beats all other competitors in the all-around event by five full points.

CONCLUSION: YOUR JOURNEY STARTS HERE!

YOU CAN DO IT, TOO

Just like Simone repeatedly soared over every obstacle on her way to achieving gold, you can also face your fears to make your dreams come true. When the road ahead seems impossible to cross, this may mean you need to slow down to calculate your next move.

Simone Biles battled through the pain of knee injuries and kidney stones to beat the competition. And even though she took a step back to rest her body and her mind, Simone came back stronger than ever. Being honest about her struggles with ADHD and mental health made these topics easier for others to talk about. She is living proof that when you set your goals, no matter what stands in your way, you can still win.

KEEP REACHING FOR THE STARS

Persistence Pays Off: Simone's story underscores the value of perseverance and hard work in the face of adversity. She continues to make a difference in children's lives by giving back to her community and speaking openly about issues that affect anyone who struggles with mental health.

Overcoming Obstacles: Setbacks are part of the journey and can be overcome with determination. Several times in her career, Simone proved that she was more than just a small gymnast. She was a powerful, talented athlete who trained tirelessly and fiercely outperformed her competition in spite of any physical or mental pain she battled.

Embracing Individuality: Simone's story should encourage you to be true to who you are and to celebrate everyone's unique qualities. Simone never asked for stardom, but she forged a path that was all her own making. This Inspirational tale can serve as a guide as you blaze a bright future of your own making.

The first step to a backflip is taking that first step. Get out there and set your dreams in motion!

Glossary

Advocacy: Publicly talking about supporting a cause.

Agility: Moving your body with ease.

Champion: This can be a person who is undefeated (like in sports or other competitions) or who gets the highest score. It also can mean someone who speaks up for others.

Collage: A collage is a collection of images (printed, painted, cut from magazines, or other locations) that creates a cohesive art piece to reflect a single connected theme.

Diagnosis: When all the symptoms an individual has point to an illness, disease, or disorder, the illness, disease, or disorder is the diagnosis.

Empathetic: Showing compassion and understanding for others.

Gymnastics: A sport that requires a person to physically train their body in areas of agility, coordination, balance, and flexibility that often includes the use of rhythmic music, a balance beam, parallel bars, uneven bars, and other equipment.

Hiatus: A pause or break.

Hydrotherapy: This physical therapy technique uses a pool of water to help a patient's muscles relax and heal.

Iconic: A signature move or symbol that is unique to a famous person can be considered iconic; when a person is iconic, they are famous or well-respected.

Merit: A system for determining the value of a performer's work

Olympics: A set of athletic events where competitors from around the world test their skills in areas such as swimming, ice skating, gymnastics, running, baseball, and many more. Each participant trains for years to become the best in their specific sport before trying to compete on an Olympic team against others who have trained hard, too.

Resilient: Bouncing back and continuing on when you are faced with difficulties.

Routine: In gymnastics, this can be a timed performance using gym equipment or when an individual performs acrobatics on the floor exercise. It includes athletic displays and skills, usually set to music.

References:

Armour, N. (2023, October 7). Simone Biles vault final shows athlete safety doesn't matter to FIG at world championships. USA Today. https://www.usatoday.com/story/sports/olympics/2023/10/07/simone-biles-event-finals-day-1-live-gymnastics-world-championships/71090324007

Bannon's Gymnastix. (2016, July 30). The Olympians: From 1964 to 2020. https://theolympians.co/tag/bannons-gymnastix

Biles, S. (2023). About. Simone Biles. https://simonebiles.com/about

Biles wows with golds on beam, floor; Young scores second silver as U.S. wraps up thrilling World Championships. (2023, October 8). USA Gymnastics. https://usagym.org/biles-wows-with-golds-on-beam-floor-young-scores-second-silver-as-u-s-wraps-up-thrilling-world-championships/#:~:text=ANTWERP%2C%20Belgium%20%E2%80%93%20Simone%20Biles%20(,Worlds%20for%20the%20U.S.%20men

Bregman, S. (2023, August 5). Simone Biles back on top with all-around win at the 2023 U.S. Classic. Olympics. https://olympics.com/en/news/simone-biles-win-2023-us-classic-core-hydration-results-paris-2024

Disciplines Women's Artistic: Simone Biles. (2023). USA Gymnastics. https://members.usagym.org/pages/athletes/nationalTeamWomen.html?id=164887

Escobar, S. (2021, July 15). 15 fun facts that will make you love Simone Biles even more. Good Housekeeping. https://www.goodhousekeeping.com/life/inspirational-stories/news/g3779/who-is-simone-biles

Halson, S. L. (2014, January). Recovery techniques for athletes. Gatorade Sports Science Institute. https://www.gssiweb.org/sports-science-exchange/article/sse-120-recovery-techniques-for-athletes#:~:text=Some%20of%20the%20most%20popular,%2C%20massage%2C%20sleep%20and%20nutrition.

How many kids are in foster care in the US?. (2023, August 23). USA Facts. https://usafacts.org/articles/how-many-kids-are-in-foster-care

Igoe, K. J. (2021, July 28). 16 Simone Biles quotes to forever be inspired by. Marie Claire. https://www.marieclaire.com/culture/a37146629/simone-biles-quotes

Kogi, C. (2023, January 10). 20 of the most inspiring Simone Biles quotes about life. Sports Brief. https://sportsbrief.com/athletics/31731-20-inspiring-simone-biles-quotes-life

Nardino, M. (2023, March 14). Simone Biles' most honest quotes about mental health and wellness through the years: 'We're human'. US Weekly. https://www.usmagazine.com/celebrity-news/pictures/simone-biles-most-honest-quotes-about-mental-health-wellness

Official website of Simone Biles. (2013, March 6). Web Archive. https://web.archive.org/web/20130306071629/http://www.gym-style.com/simonebiles/about.htm

Olympic Games - Summer, Winter, YOG, & Paralympics. (2023). Olympics. https://olympics.com/en/olympic-games

Powers, H. (2023, April 2). How much practice is too much or too little?. All Gymnasts. https://allgymnasts.com/much-practice-much-little

Praderio, C. (2018, October 28). Simone Biles is dominating at the gymnastics world championships despite having a kidney stone that sent her to the ER. Insider. https://www.insider.com/simone-biles-kidney-stone-world-championships-2018-10#:~:text=Biles%20explained%20that%20she%20was,with%20the%20pain%20later!'

Reynolds, M. (2016, August 11). Simone Biles: 'I'm not the next Usain Bolt or Michael Phelps. I'm the first Simone Biles'. Jezebel. https://jezebel.com/simone-biles-im-not-the-next-usain-bolt-or-michael-ph-1785182242?utm_campaign=socialflow_jezebel_facebook&utm_source=jezebel_facebook&utm_medium=socialflow

Rodulfo, K. (2016, August 11). Simone Biles would like you to not compare her to male athletes. Elle. https://www.elle.com/culture/news/a38468/simone-biles-im-not-the-next-usain-bolt-michael-phelps

Simone Biles. (2023). Olympics. https://olympics.com/en/athletes/simone-biles

Simone Biles: Gymnast and Olympic gold medalist. (2023, October 6). Academy of Achievement. https://achievement.org/achiever/simone-biles/#:~:text=On%20a%20daycare%20field%20trip,child%20take%20regular%20gymnastic%20classes.

Simone Biles presented with the Presidential Medal of Freedom. (2022, July 18). Friends of the Children. https://friendsofthechildren.org/news/simone-biles-presented-with-the-presidential-medal-of-freedom

Thompson, E. (2023, August 27). Simone Biles and Jonathan Owens' relationship timeline. US Weekly. https://www.usmagazine.com/celebrity-news/pictures/simone-biles-and-jonathan-owens-relationship-timeline

Walcott, E. (2023, October 14). Simone Biles says she is 'speechless' and 'honored' at having 5th gymnastics skill named after her. Yahoo! News. https://www.yahoo.com/entertainment/simone-biles-says-she-speechless-143117762.html

Walker, N. (2018, November 13). Simone Biles gives foster kids a 'ticket to dream'. NBC DFW. https://www.nbcdfw.com/news/local/simone-biles-gives-foster-kids-a-ticket-to-dream/226178

Made in United States
Cleveland, OH
03 December 2024